The DOG LOVERS' Guides

Shih Tzu

Shih Tzu

By Pat Lord

Mason Crest
450 Parkway Drive, Suite D
Broomall, PA 19008
www.masoncrest.com

Series ISBN: 978-1-4222-3848-6
Hardback ISBN: 978-1-4222-3861-5
EBook ISBN: 978-1-4222-7940-3

First printing
1 3 5 7 9 8 6 4 2

Cover photograph by Chaoss/Dreamstime.com.

Library of Congress Cataloging-in-Publication Data is on file with the publisher.

QR Codes disclaimer:

You may gain access to certain third-party content ("Third-Party Sites") by scanning and using the QR Codes that appear in this publication (the "QR Codes"). We do not operate or control in any respect any information, products, or services on such Third-Party Sites linked to by us via the QR Codes included in this publication, and we assume no responsibility for any materials you may access using the QR Codes. Your use of the QR Codes may be subject to terms, limitations, or restrictions set forth in the applicable terms of use or otherwise established by the owners of the Third-Party Sites. Our linking to such Third-Party Sites via the QR Codes does not imply an endorsement or sponsorship of such Third-Party Sites, or the information, products, or services offered on or through the Third-Party Sites, nor does it imply an endorsement or sponsorship of this publication by the owners of such Third-Party Sites.

MAY 2018

Contents

Key Icons to Look For

Sidebars: This boxed material within the main text allows readers to build knowledge, gain insights, explore possibilities, and broaden their perspectives by weaving together additional information to provide realistic and holistic perspectives.

Educational Videos: Readers can view videos by scanning our QR codes, providing them with additional educational content to supplement the text. Examples include news coverage, moments in history, speeches, iconic moments, and much more!

Series Glossary of Key Terms: This back-of-the-book glossary contains terminology used throughout this series. Words found here increase the reader's ability to read and comprehend higher-level books and articles in this field.

Chapter 1

Introducing the Shih Tzu

Although this dog comes in a small package, the Shih Tzu considers himself to be a big dog. With his superb temperament, character, and good looks, it is easy to understand how this little dog can steal your heart away.

The Shih Tzu (pronounced *SHEE-dzoo;* the plural is also Shih Tzu) was bred primarily as a companion, and you could not wish for a better friend and playmate. He is so adaptable, suited to town or country, prepared to rest quietly by your chair, romp in the yard, or enjoy long country walks. A close friend thought I was somewhat eccentric when I referred to one of my Shih Tzu as a "little person"— that is, until the lady owned one! The Shih Tzu is so tuned in to his humans that it is astonishing, and for me and many others who have the pleasure of owning these little dogs, there is no better companion.

Here we have a breed that is, thankfully, born without many health problems. We are lucky that the Shih Tzu is a relatively long-

lived breed, and, with luck, will live well into double figures. Still, he is not the dog of choice for everyone.

The Shih Tzu has a long coat, which looks stunning when it is properly cared for, but demands a huge amount of time and commitment. The Shih Tzu coat requires daily attention, and grooming your dog needs to be an established—and enjoyable—part of your day. Of course, you can keep your dog in a pet trim—although that still requires regular brushing. Clearly, this is not a breed for someone who wants to cut corners with coat care.

The Shih Tzu thrives on company, and he will pine if he is left for long periods on his own. He is certainly not suited to living outdoors—or even spending a large part of the day there. He needs to be inside with his people.

He is a happy, endearing companion, and although easy to train, he has a mind of his own. So training is definitely a must.

Shih Tzu temperament

First and foremost, the Shih Tzu adores people; he has the knack of being very attentive without being too fussy or demanding. He is good with children, and will be more than happy to join in their games. He is alert but certainly not yappy, as he is far too intelligent to waste time and energy on unnecessary barking. He gets along well with other dogs and animals of all sizes. Shih Tzu also have an uncanny ability to recognize their own breed; once you own one, you will find it a great temptation to make it two!

The Shih Tzu is an active dog who loves to play, especially with soft toys. The independent streak means he can amuse himself for hours with dog toys—or sleep happily in the security of his own home. In terms of exercise, the adaptable Shih Tzu will enjoy as much as he is given.

Tracing back in time

The Shih Tzu is one of several breeds originating in Tibet and China that were intended to look like little lions. It's hard to separate the origins of the Shih Tzu, Pekingese (pictured here), and Lhasa Apso, and centuries ago they were probably not distinct breeds.

During the Ming Dynasty (1368–1644), these dogs became favored pets of the royal family, and there are ancient scrolls with pictures of these lion dogs. (Eunuchs were charged with breeding a variety of these dogs).

At the same time, lion dogs were being bred in the temples of Tibet. Statues of these holy dogs were placed to guard the entrances to Buddhist temples.

Lion dogs were exchanged between the royal palace in Beijing and the temples of Tibet. During the Qing Dynasty (1644–1912), the Dalai Lama (the spiritual and political leader of Tibet) sent a pair of Shih Tzu as a gift to Empress Cixi when she came to power in 1861. The dogs quickly became her favorite among all her breeds of little lions, and she appointed her chief eunuch to oversee the breeding program. She also insisted that he keep complete pedigrees and descriptions of all markings on all dogs used for breeding.

Chaos in China

Breeding was confined to the palace, and gifts of royal Shih Tzu were much coveted among foreign diplomats. By the early 1900s, a few had been obtained by Europeans.

After Cixi died in 1908, the palace eunuchs became careless with their breeding programs, and there doubtless were mixes with other types of lion dogs in the royal kennels. They also began selling Shih Tzu on the black market. When the Qing Dynasty was overthrown in 1912 and replaced with a republic, the royal kennels were disbanded.

In 1923,, the China Kennel Club was formed in Shanghai and classed all small lion dogs as either Lhasa Terriers or Tibetan Poodles. In 1934, the Peking Kennel Club called them all Lhasa Lion Dogs, and separated them by dogs over and under 12 pounds (5.4 kg). The Shih Tzu breed was no longer firmly established in its homeland. After the Communist revolution in 1949, purebred dog breeding came to an end.

Coming to the West

Meanwhile, Shih Tzu from the foundation stock of the palace in Beijing ended up in Europe, brought there by diplomats. These dogs included three imported by Lady Brownrigg in Great Britain for her Taishan kennel, and six other imports, which came into the U.K. between 1933 and 1959.

Dogopedia: Shih Tzu

British foundation stock included two additional dogs, Aidzo and Leidza, who were both given to the Queen Mother in 1933. These dogs came from Mrs. Henrik Kauffman of Denmark, although they were both born in Beijing.

In Britain the breed was

known as Tibetan Lion Dogs, but the Kennel Club classed them as Lhasa Apsos and they were shown in the same ring. In 1934 the Kennel Club ruled that dogs from Tibet were Apsos and those from China were a separate breed, now known by their Chinese name: Shih Tzu. (Shih Tzu is an Anglicized version of Shi Zi Gou, which is Chinese for "little lion dog.")

The infamous Pekingese cross

During World War II, most breeding programs suffered greatly across Europe. After the war, as dog breeders struggled to recover, Shih Tzu breeders faced a special problem: There were very few purebred Shih Tzu to breed from in Europe, and none could be im-

ported from China because of the revolution. Faults were creeping in, and many felt the breed was becoming to big, too leggy, plain in the face, and not quite as sweet in temperament.

In 1952, a top Pekingese breeder, Elfreda Evans, mated a black Shih Tzu bitch, Elfann Fenling of Yram, to a black and white Pekingese male, Philadelphus Suti-T'sun of Elfann. She had heard that the Chinese emperors bred their little lion dogs to Pekingese every few generations, and decided it was not a bad idea. Scandal ensued.

The puppies were not considered purebred and could not be registered. In fact, the Kennel Club would only register puppies four generations after the cross. And since almost all the important American lines came from British imports, American breeders had to wait even longer for full American Kennel Club (AKC) recognition.

Coming to America

When the Shih Tzu was first imported into America in the late 1930s, there were similar problems with establishing the breed's identity. Shih Tzu were not recognized by the AKC as a separate breed. At that time, the majority of the imports were made by army personnel who had come across the breed while stationed in Great Britain or Scandinavia. The dogs they brought home were shown and bred as Lhasa Apsos, until the Shih Tzu was officially recognized by the AKC in 1955—but only in the Miscellaneous Class.

Maureen Murdock and Philip Price, her nephew, were the first to import and breed recognized, pedigreed Shih Tzu in the United States. In 1954 Price went to the U.K. and brought back to Philadelphia Golden S. Wen of Chasmu; the following year he imported Ho Lai of Yram.

In 1957 the Shih Tzu Club of America was formed in the eastern part of the United States. By 1960 there were three Shih Tzu clubs, and by 1961 there were over 100 Shih Tzu registered. In 1963, the Shih Tzu Club of America and the Texas Shih Tzu Society merged to form the American Shih Tzu Club. In 1969, the Shih Tzu finally got full AKC recognition.

Ingrid Colwell was another important breeder in the United States. She moved to Pennsylvania from Sweden with her American husband, taking with her five purebred Shih Tzu. These dogs included French Ch. Jungfaltets Jung-Wu and two from the Pukedals kennel, which had been her mother's in Sweden. Colwell imported several more Shih Tzu from Britain and Scandinavia, and in total, bred 79 Shih Tzu.

Worldwide favorite

Currently the Shih Tzu is the twentieth-most popular breed registered with the AKC and among the top 20 most popular toy breed dogs in the world.

Zsa Zsa Gabor was a well-known and highly respected Shih Tzu breeder for many years. Former Spice Girl Geri Halliwell made sure a likeness of her Shih Tzu, Harry, stands beside her in the famed Madame Tussauds wax museum in London. Nicole Richie, Susie Essman, Oleg Cassini, Bill Gates, Mariah Carey, Beyoncé, Jane Seymour, Colin Farell, and Vidal Sassoon are among the rich and famous who have been captivated by this delightful breed.

Chapter 2

What Should a Shih Tzu Look Like?

The breed standard is a written blueprint describing not only the physical appearance, but also the ideal temperament and characteristics that should typify a particular breed.

Every breed has a breed standard, which is drawn up by the national breed club. The aim is to give guidance on the essentials of the breed, and to protect it from exaggerations that could be detrimental to the health of the animal.

General appearance

The breed standard starts with an overall impression of the breed—but there is an important factor to consider. The breed standard has been written for a Shih Tzu in full coat. As you will see from

the many photographs in this book, there is a significant difference in general appearance between a dog in full coat and one who has been clipped or trimmed—although we are dealing with the same dog underneath.

The breed standard asks for a sturdy dog, by this it means a dog with physical substance, not a fragile toy breed. The standard also says, "Befitting his noble Chinese ancestry as a highly valued, prized companion and palace pet, the Shih Tzu is proud of bearing, has a distinctively arrogant carriage with head well up and tail curved over the back."

Throughout the breed standard, proportion takes precedence over any individual part. It is essential that all aspects of the dog are in proportion, and that no part appears exaggerated.

Size

The breed standard gives quite a wide scope to this sturdy little dog. The ideal height at the withers (the top point of the shoulder) is 9 to 10.5 inches (24 to 25 cm). In any case, a Shih Tzu should not be less than 8 inches (20 cm) nor more than 11 inches (28 cm). Ideally, the weight of a mature dog is 9 to 16 pounds (4 to 7.25 kg). More important than size, though, is proportion.

Head and skull

The head is round and broad, with a good space between the eyes. As the Shih Tzu grows from a puppy, so does the coat, beard, and whiskers—the hair growing upwards and outwards from the muzzle. This pattern of growth helps to give the breed its distinct chrysanthemum-like face. Although not specifically mentioned in the standard, a chrysanthemum-like face is a feature of the breed. Imagine the biggest bloom you have ever seen on a chry-

santhemum, with each petal delicately folded into the next. This is a metaphor for the glorious round head of a Shih Tzu—covered in long, flowing hair—which you can cup gently between your hands.

This chrysanthemum-like face is particularly striking in young-sters, before the hair becomes too heavy and needs to be tied up. Obviously, this hair growth should not damage the dog's eyes or affect her vision—which is why the hair is tied up in a topknot.

The muzzle should be of ample width, square and short; it should be flat and hairy with no evidence of wrinkles. The front of the muzzle should be flat, nor pointy. The width and padding of the muzzle can make a vast difference to the soft expression required by the breed standard.

The muzzle should be about one inch (2.5 cm) from the tip of the nose to the definite stop between the eyes (the place where the muzzle meets the skull). The muzzle should be level, but a slight up-tilt is allowed.

The Shih Tzu's delightful nose should be black, but liver or blue on dogs with marking in those colors is permissible. Pink is never allowed. Wide open nostrils are asked for, to help avoid breathing problems.

In general, the standard says, the expression should be, "Warm, sweet, wide-eyed, friendly and trusting. An overall well-balanced and pleasant expression supersedes the importance of individual parts."

Eyes

The large, dark, round eyes should be placed well apart. I cannot emphasize enough how essential it is to have correct eyes. To look into the correct dark eyes of a Shih Tzu is to see the entire appeal of the dog. Their warm, trusting expression can make you glow, even on a cold, damp day!

The eyes should not be so large as to be prominent, or bulbous, as they could be easily damaged if this was the case. Lighter colored eyes are only permitted in liver or blue marked dogs, and no white of eye should be visible.

Ears

The ears should be large and set below the crown of the skull. In a fully coated dog the ears actually appear larger than they are, due to the wealth of hair covering them.

Mouth

This is wide and slightly undershot. An undershot bite is when the outer surface of the upper teeth engages or nearly engages the inner surface of the lower teeth.

Forequarters

The neck should be well proportioned, and nicely arched, to carry the head proudly. This contributes to the arrogant look associated with this breed.

The shoulders should be well laid back, referring to the angle of the shoulder blades. The shoulders should not be excessively heavy, but should flow smoothly from the neck to the shoulder.

The front legs should be set well apart and under the chest. They should be muscular, sturdy, and as straight as possible, with the feet pointing forward. Shih Tzu should not have what's known as a fiddle front, where the front legs bow out like the shape of a violin.

Body

The dog should be slightly longer than she is tall, and should never look leggy or squat. The depth of the rib cage should extend to just below the elbows; the distance from elbows to withers is a little greater than from elbows to ground. The chest is broad and deep but not overloaded like a barrel. There should be a good spring of rib, so the dog does not look flat or slab-sided (narrow). The topline is level.

Hindquarters

The hind legs should be short, sturdy, and muscular, straight when viewed from the rear. The thighs are well rounded and muscular. Therefore, the hindquarters will need to be in proportion to the forequarters to

Pros and cons of Shih Tzus

achieve the correct balance. The feet are round and well padded; it could be said that they cushion the movement of the dog. They are usually well covered in hair.

Tail

In a fully coated dog, the tail is another feature of the Shih Tzu that adds to her glory. The heavily-plumed tail should be set high on the rump, and carried in curve well over the back—in fact, carried at a height approximately level with that of the skull to give a balanced outline. In a really good example, it should be difficult to tell which end is which! A tail carried flat on the dog's back, curly, or set low, will totally detract from the overall balance and outline of the dog.

Coat Colors

Shih Tzu come in an array of solid colors and in combinations of two or three colors. A white blaze on the forehead, right between the eyes, and a white tip at the end of the tail are highly prized. It has been said that the Chinese eunuchs who bred Shih Tzu in the temples considered these to be especially lucky dogs.

All the colors come in a variety of shades, so often it's up to the breeder to just pick a color category for pup. A coat may darken or lighten as a puppy matures, as well.

Black and white

Black, gold, and white

Brindle and white

Red and white

Gait/movement

Gait is another word for stride or movement. If a dog meets the structural requirements of the breed standard, her movement should be smooth and flowing. A Shih Tzu should move with ease, floating along proudly and elegantly. She needs to be able to reach well forward from the front, and have the same strong power from the rear. You should see the full black pads from the hind feet as she moves away.

This movement is truly a glorious sight to see in a well-constructed Shih Tzu—like a ship in full sail. However, if any part of the anatomy is incorrect, out of proportion or out of balance, then something is likely to break down.

Coat

For a show dog, a full coat is required. The outer coat is long, dense, and not curly, with moderate undercoat that is not woolly. A slight wave to the coat is permitted.

The hair should not affect the dog's ability to see, and length of coat should not restrict movement.

Trimming is allowed only on the feet, bottom of the coat, and around the anus for neatness.

Colors

The Shih Tzu comes in a very wide array of colors and combinations. The solid colors are far less common, and

typically you will see dogs with more than one color. However, the breed standard recognizes all colors and markings, and says all are to be considered equally.

When registering a Shih Tzu puppy, breeders typically pick from eight solid colors. Black, white, gold, red, and silver (shiny gray) refer to a single color on the coat. Brindle, although listed as a solid color, is actually a combination of a white base coat with streaking. The solid colors liver and blue are actually based on the skin pigmentation on the nose, paws, and eye rims—the coat may be any color at all.

There are seven recognized mixtures of two colors. All have white as the base, so it's white and black, blue, brindle, gold, liver, red, or silver.

Finally, there are four recognized tricolor combinations: silver, gold and white; black, silver and white; black, gold and white; and black, silver and gold.

Temperament

The Shih Tzu is described as being intelligent, active and alert, with a friendly and independent temperament. This sums up the endearing small sized, huge hearted, little dog. You will find that the Shih Tzu simply overflows with character and intelligence; in fact, she is usually one step ahead of you.

On this topic the breed standard says, "As the sole purpose of the Shih Tzu is that of a companion and house pet, it is essential that its temperament be outgoing, happy, affectionate, friendly and trusting toward all."

The Shih Tzu is a wonderful breed in so many ways, and is the ideal companion for so many people. It is in the hands of our judges and breeders to make sure that Shih Tzu retain all their qualities, especially their marvelous character, temperament, and good health.

Chapter 3

What Do You Want from Your Shih Tzu?

The Shih Tzu is a wonderful breed and a marvelous pet, but you must make sure you know exactly what you want from your dog, so your dreams of dog ownership match the reality.

Show dog

If you have ambitions to exhibit your Shih Tzu in the show ring, your requirements will be very different from the average pet owner. The need for a healthy dog, of sound temperament, must be paramount (as it is for all dog owners), but you will also need to find a puppy who conforms as closely as possible to the breed standard. If you have your heart set on a particular color or combination, it may take longer to find a suitable puppy.

Bear in mind that exhibiting a Shih Tzu in the show ring is an entirely different prospect than owning one as a pet. There is so much time, care, and attention required to keep up that full show coat.

Unfortunately, this is not a breed that you can decide to show one minute and not the next, because like any beauty pageant—and let us face it, that is exactly what dog showing is—your exhibit requires daily beauty therapy and attention.

Companion dog

The adaptable Shih Tzu is a delightful pet for people of all ages. He will be a devoted companion for a couple or a person living on their own, and he will be a fun playmate for families, particularly those with slightly older children, who will be more appreciative and considerate of his needs.

He is also a good choice for seniors, because his exercise needs are moderate. He will enjoy short outings, as long as he also has the opportunity to putter around in a yard or dog run.

Watchdog

The Shih Tzu can be quite a vocal breed, particularly when he hears strangers approaching. His distant ancestors were kept as watchdogs in the temples of Tibet, and the Shih Tzu of today is alert to all comings and goings. However, if you want a dog to guard your home, think again. A Shih Tzu will bark when a burglar approaches, but is more likely to show the intruder around the house than to chase him off!

What does your Shih Tzu want from you?

As well as deciding what you want from your Shih Tzu, you need to think what he wants from you, and whether you are able to provide it.

Socialization

Socializing puppies is vital if you want well-adjusted adults. In his lifetime, your Shih Tzu will encounter a wide variety of people and a wide range of situations, and he may have to adapt to many different places. You need to prepare him for this by working out a program of socialization from puppyhood through adulthood.

You want a dog who is happy to meet and greet people of all ages, regardless of whether they are friends or strangers, who will interact peaceably with other dogs, and who takes the sights and sounds of the modern world in stride. Only by exposing your Shih Tzu to all these experiences will he learn to react calmly and with confidence.

There are so many places you can take your puppy to make sure he meets lots of people and other dogs. Go to the local park, or perhaps tuck your puppy under your arm and visit a flea market or a local street fair. A Shih Tzu puppy, like many puppies, is simply irresistible to everyone, and you will find that people will not be able to contain themselves and will just have to stop and chat with you both—which all helps with the puppy's socializing.

Training

You may think a small dog, such as a Shih Tzu, does not need training—but you would be making a big mistake. All dogs, regardless of size or breed, need some training so they have good manners at home and out and about, and so they understand what you expect of them.

There are other benefits associated with training your dog.

• A well-behaved dog is a joy to take anywhere.

• You will enjoy teaching your dog, and he will enjoy using his brain to learn new things.

• Training builds a strong bond between you both.

• You will make lots of new friends while training and socializing your dog.

• Dogs enjoy having clear rules and boundaries, sensibly applied.

• Everyone benefits from having a well-trained dog: you, your family, friends, neighbors, and your community.

Love and understanding

A Shih Tzu thrives on companionship, and he will repay you with his own very special brand of loyalty and affection. There is no doubt that you will love your little dog—it is almost impossible not to—but you must go one step further and try to understand him.

Work at reading your Shih Tzu's body language; this is a strong indicator of how he is feeling. For example, the tail of a Shih Tzu can tell you much about his mental and physical condition, because it acts like a sign.

If at any time your Shih Tzu is on the move and his tail is down, something is wrong. The most common reason is that he feels insecure, wary, or even nervous of someone or something. As soon as he considers the danger or problem has passed, up will come that tail.

The dropped tail carriage can also give you an indication that he is unwell, in pain, or he may even have hurt his tail. But remember this only applies when he is on the move, not when he is resting.

This is just one example of "reading" your dog, but it shows how important it is to tune in to his feelings so that you can react accordingly and safeguard his health and well-being. Note that Shih Tzu have a very low pain threshold and will become noticeably very depressed. If your dog ever becomes unwell, he will require plenty of tender loving care.

Other considerations

Now you have decided the Shih Tzu is the breed for you, the next step is to narrow the choices, so you know exactly what you are looking for.

Male or female?

In general, the Shih Tzu has such a laid-back, relaxed temperament that—besides the obvious difference—there is not much to separate the male and female. Although both sexes can be strong-willed, there is no great difference between the boys and girls in this regard.

Males

The male is a happy, fun-loving little chap and is definitely as affectionate, if not slightly more so, than the female. He will reach puberty at quite a young age, and is therefore capable of siring puppies from as young as eight and a half months. Do not be fooled by his young puppy look; just bear in mind what he is capable of, especially if you have an unspayed female.

Neutering a male is a sensible option for pet owners. However, this is a matter of choice and should be discussed with your veterinarian. If you do have your dog neutered, be sure to watch his weight carefully as, due to the hormonal changes, he will need fewer calories to maintain his weight. An overweight dog is an unhealthy dog.

If you are intending to show your dog, a male is probably slightly easier to own in some respects because he does not have the six-monthly hormone change, as females in season do, and is therefore less likely to lose his coat.

Females

The female, like the male, is also full of fun—a sweet-natured companion just as anxious to love and be loved. It is normal for her to come into season for the first time anywhere between 6 and 12 months, and every six months thereafter. However, in some bloodlines, bitches only come into season every 12 months. A season lasts for 21 to 28 days, and during this time, a female must be kept separate from all male dogs. Great care must be taken if you go out for ex-

ercise, and she must be secure and safe in your yard.

If your female Shih Tzu is going to be purely a pet—not exhibited or bred after her show career—it would be more advantageous for her to be spayed.

The female does not need to have a litter of puppies for the sake of her health or well-being. In fact, there are health benefits to spaying, as it will eliminate the risk of conditions such as pyometra (a serious uterine infection) and mammary cancer.

Your veterinarian will advise you about spaying, which is usually done before a bitch comes into season the first time. Females also need fewer calories after spaying, so always bear this in mind.

More than one?

Resist the temptation to get two puppies from the same litter, or two of similar ages, because all your time will be needed to look after one puppy.

Early training is essential if your puppy is to grow up to be a loving and well-mannered member of your family, but this does not happen overnight. It is far better to take on one puppy, which will enable you to stick to a daily routine of handling, grooming, socializing, feeding, housetraining, and general manners training.

Once you have fallen in love with the breed and think you might like to have more than one, you will find that your first dog will take great delight in helping you to train the new addition. However, it is extremely difficult to housetrain two puppies at the same time.

Shih Tzu are very sociable dogs and they adore the company of their own breed. It is possible to have a pair of well-trained males or females together without any problem. If you want a pair of different sexes, spay and neuter both and they will be fine.

An older dog will accept a youngster coming in, but careful introduction is required, as a youngster can be rather exuberant.

Adult or rescued dogs

You may wish to skip the puppy stage and take on an adult dog—maybe one who has retired from breeding, lost his owner, or a rescued dog who needs a new home. There are Shih Tzu rescue groups that can be found through breed clubs. (You'll find some information in the Find Out More section of this book.)

When providing a home for an adult dog, especially a rescue, do remember that there may well be some problems to start with. The dog may be used to an entirely different lifestyle; he may be poorly socialized or not housetrained; he may be nervous around strangers due to lack of companionship. The more you know about the dog's history, the easier it will be to help him adjust to his new life, but always remember that kindness, patience, and understanding are essential.

Chapter 4

Finding Your Puppy

I t is so easy to look at lovely, fluffy puppies and fall for the first one you see. But has the breeder given them a good start in life? The time, care, and thought that goes into planning and rearing a litter will have a huge impact on the future well-being of the puppies that are produced.

Essentially, you are looking for a clean, happy, healthy, friendly puppy who is typical of the breed and is likely to live to a ripe old age. To avoid unnecessary heartache, it is best to be patient and find the right puppy for you, from the right source.

Responsible breeders

Responsible breeders raise their puppies at home and underfoot. They have one or, at the most, two litters at a time. They carefully study the pedigrees of the male and female before they arrange any breeding, with an eye toward breeding the healthiest, most temper-

amentally sound Shih Tzu. Responsible breeders belong to a breed club and are involved in their breed.

Responsible breeders register their puppies with a well-established registry such as the American Kennel Club or the United Kennel Club. (Registration with a well-established kennel club is a guarantee that your Shih Tzu is truly a Shih Tzu, but it is not a guarantee of good health or temperament.) They are able to hand over registration documents at the time of sale. Their breeding dogs are permanently identified by microchip or DNA. They screen them for hereditary health problems, and can tell you exactly which screening tests their dogs have had and what the results were.

You should be able to meet the mother and see where the puppies are kept. Everything should look and smell clean and healthy. The mother should be a well-socialized dog. She may be a little protective of her babies, but she should act like a typical Shih Tzu.

Responsible breeders socialize all their puppies in a home environment. They provide written advice on feeding, on-going training, socialization, parasite control, and vaccinations. They are available for phone calls after you buy their puppies, and will take a dog back at any time. They have a written contract of sale for each puppy that conforms to your state's laws.

Picking a puppy

Finding a responsible breeder

A good starting place is to go to dog shows, where you will be able to see a variety of Shih Tzu of different types and colors. Wait until a class has been judged, and then talk to the exhibitors—particularly if you have seen a dog you really like the look of. Ask questions about the dog's breeding, and her temperament; this is a valuable way of gaining more information about the breed.

The exhibitors you talk to may or may not know about upcoming litters, but if they are not able to help, you can do some more research on the national breed club website (listed in Find Out More).

Bear in mind that responsible breeders usually breed a litter when they want a new puppy to show, and therefore, there may be a waiting list.

Buyer beware!

In your impatience to find a Shih Tzu puppy, it is all too easy to fall into the trap of going to an unsuitable source.

Avoid newspapers advertising a litter, or cards placed in store windows. At best, these could be the result of an inexperienced pet owner breeding a litter, and although they may have done a good job, there are absolutely no guarantees—particularly regarding the choice of a sire. All too often, the neighborhood dog will have been chosen as a good match, without any research into bloodlines and health issues.

Be especially wary of advertising on the Internet. Just having a website does not make someone a responsible breeder. There is also a danger that the puppies may have come from a puppy farm, where litters of all breeds are produced purely for financial gain, with no thought as to the health, temperament, or rearing of the puppies involved.

Recommendations from breed clubs, veterinarians, and people who have already bought from a particular breeder are usually much more reliable.

Questions, questions

When looking for a Shih Tzu, make sure you know what you want, how much you are willing to pay, and that you have researched the health and requirements of the breed. If you find a breeder you are interested in, phone and ask as many questions as you need to; a reputable breeder will be only too pleased to provide you with as much information as you require.

Ask where the puppies are being reared, and how they are being socialized and housetrained. Check the health status of the parents. Like all breeds, the Shih Tzu has some inherited conditions, and you need to

ensure the breeder has the necessary checks and clearances on the litter's mother and father.

The breeder will also have lots of questions for you. These may include:

- Who is in your family? If you have children, how old are they?
- Will someone be home during the day to look after the puppy?
- Do you have a securely fenced yard?
- Do you have plans to show your puppy?

Do not be offended by the barrage of questions. Responsible breeders take seriously their responsibility for every puppy they produce, and that's a good thing.

Puppy watching

No sensible breeder should allow anyone to visit puppies until they are on their feet and starting to play and run around, which is generally at five to six weeks of age. The puppies should be reared in the house and be living in clean and comfortable surroundings. Puppies obviously do make a mess and are not housetrained at this stage of their life, but there should be no excessive odor from them or the environment in which they are kept.

They should have clean coats and bright eyes, with no discharge, and their rear ends should also be clean and free from any signs of matting or diarrhea. Their nostrils should be clear and not pinched, causing any difficulty in breathing. You also need to check that there are no umbilical or groin hernias (look around the navel), which are sometimes seen in Shih Tzu, and would require surgery.

The puppies should be brought up in an environment that allows them to become accustomed to household noises, such as voices, television, radio, vacuum cleaner, and washing machine. This is all part of socializing them. It is imperative that this takes place at an early stage of their life, as this is when their characters are developing.

The pups should also be handled gently and often by the breeder and family, to prepare them for what is to come. If the puppies are not socialized early on, it can result in nervous puppies who cannot cope with loud noises and with strangers, and this nervousness can stay with them forever.

You should be able to meet the mother of the puppies, although, depending on the age of the puppies, she may not be with them constantly once they have started to eat solid food. The dam should also be in a clean and healthy condition, friendly and happy to greet you.

It is not uncommon for the father or sire of the puppies not to be owned by the breeder, as breeders do not keep several stud dogs at one time. However, the breeder will advise you what recognition he may have in the show ring, making him worthy of being used at stud.

When you visit the puppies they should be full of life, running around playing with one another, responding immediately to your arrival. There should be no sign of nervousness or holding back—there is usually a rush to see which of the littermates reaches you first!

Picking a show puppy

If you want to find a puppy with show potential, it is a good idea to take an experienced person with you who understands the finer points of the breed standard.

Shih Tzu puppies are starting to shape up nicely around six weeks, but the best time to choose a show puppy is as near to eight weeks as possible, because what you see at eight weeks is the construction, outline, and balance of what that puppy is going to look like as an adult.

All puppies go through growing stages and can change considerably during that time, but if you are patient, then generally what they were at eight weeks, they will be as an adult.

It is so easy to be carried away by how cute the puppies are when you first see them. All dogs have faults—no dog is perfect—but, for example, the Shih Tzu puppy who shows white around the eyes, has small eyes, or is too short or too long in the leg, whose tail is carried too low, and so on, is already at a disadvantage when entering the show ring. However, none of these faults affect the puppy's health or prevents him in any way from becoming the most fabulous pet and companion.

Chapter 5

A Shih Tzu-Friendly Home

While you are waiting for your new puppy, there are a number of important preparations to make to get your home and your family ready for the new arrival. Your house and yard need to be puppy-proofed, you need to buy some basic equipment, and you need to agree on some house rules.

These preparations apply to any new dog you bring home, of any age. They are the means of creating an environment that is safe and secure for your Shih Tzu throughout his life.

In the home

A puppy—and even an adult dog—can get into all sorts of trouble, usually through no fault of their own. Look around and ask yourself what mischief a puppy could get up to and what he could chew. Electric cords are prime candidates, so these should be safely secured where a puppy cannot reach them. Try running exposed

cords and cables through PVC pipe to keep little teeth away. Anything breakable, such as glass or china, is very dangerous—once broken by a wagging tail, a puppy could step on sharp pieces or even swallow them. Houseplants also need to be out of reach, as, even if they are not poisonous, they will very likely upset a puppy's tummy.

When your dog comes home, you'll need to think about security all the time. Whenever you open a door or gate, remember that an inquisitive dog will soon squeeze through in search of adventure.

Take care that the puppy does not go under obstacles that may collapse on him, and he's not allowed to climb on furniture or up steps or walls, where he can so easily jump off or fall and seriously injure himself.

If there are parts of your house that are out of bounds to the new

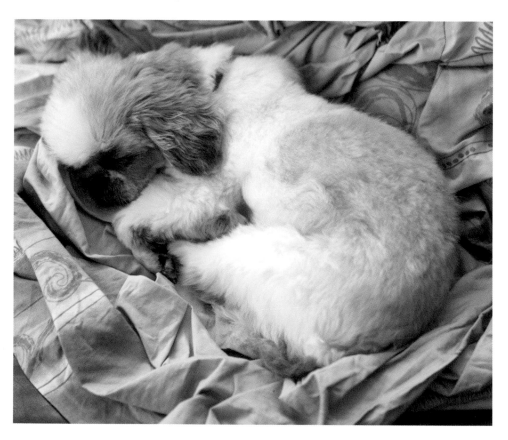

arrival, this must be made clear from the start. If you decide that your puppy is not allowed upstairs, or beyond a particular door, a baby gate will assist in keeping this rule. When using any type of barrier, be sure it is puppy-proof and that your pup cannot squeeze through, get stuck, and injure himself.

Although a puppy will run, play, and fall asleep almost anywhere, it is important that he has his own safe spot to which he can retreat. This personal space represents a place he knows he can go and feel safe, warm, and secure, and where he can rest without any interference from the family. This might be a bed or a sleeping crate in a quiet corner of the house.

Whatever house rules you have decided on, you must keep to them; otherwise, you are going to have a very confused puppy. It is very unfair and confusing for a puppy if you make one rule one minute, and then break it the next.

In the yard

The Shih Tzu is a very lively and inquisitive dog who has little sense of fear or danger—especially when he has the opportunity to investigate a whole new yard. If you are an enthusiastic gardener, there may be areas where you do not want your dog to roam. Fence them off, so your dog will never be tempted.

The most important consideration is that your yard is 100 percent safe and secure; it is amazing where a small puppy can maneuver himself. Check the gates and the fence (especially for gaps under the fence), and do not leave your puppy in the yard unsupervised.

If you have a swimming pool or a pond, you'll need to be even more careful. Ideally, the area should be fenced off as a totally no-go zone for your new addition.

Watching a Shih Tzu puppy scampering and then rolling over on the lawn will provide hours of amusement. A puppy likes nothing more than to end this energetic activity by either lying flat on his back, or with his tummy pressed against the cool grass, front legs reaching forward and hind legs stretched out behind. This may not look very comfortable, but it is a typical Shih Tzu position.

Finding a veterinarian

Do this before you bring your dog home, so you have a vet to call if there is a problem. If you do not know of a local veterinary practice, look for one close to home that deals with its own emergency calls and is happy to have small dogs in the clinic.

The vet should thoroughly check your puppy—or any new arrival—as soon as possible to give you peace of mind and also to introduce dog and vet. Animals need not be afraid of the vet, so the more enjoyable visits you can have, the better. If an emergency arises, it is important that the vet is able to handle your dog.

The vet will need to see any vaccination records and will record all the details both for you and the dog. He or she will discuss with you feeding, worming, parasite treatments, and probably microchipping, at the first visit.

Shopping for your Shih Tzu

Shopping for your Shih Tzu is fun, but before you get carried away, don't forget to pick up the essential items you will need. If you make good choices at this stage, the equipment you buy will last your Shih Tzu for many years—sometimes for a lifetime.

Indoor crate

This is an invaluable investment, providing your puppy with his own personal space—and you with peace of mind.

Make sure you buy a crate that is big enough for your dog to use when he is fully grown. If the door is left open, many adult Shih Tzu prefer their crate to a dog bed.

Puppy crate training

When introducing a crate, you want the puppy to associate it with being a safe and happy place to return to and sleep in. Never use the crate as a place of punishment. It should be used when your puppy needs to rest, when you cannot supervise him, and to keep him safe overnight. It can also be useful when you are traveling or staying in a hotel, or as a safe place to put your youngster if you have a visitor who has an allergy, or simply does not like dogs!

Dog beds

What a choice! These days we are presented with a vast array of beds for our pets. There are dog beds ranging from the typical round or oval plastic type, fur-lined beds, igloos, and even beds that look like sofas in miniature! The Shih Tzu definitely enjoys being pampered, and therefore all luxury is appropriate. However, do not be disappointed if you purchase an expensive bed and your new pet climbs out of it and stretches out full length on the carpet next to it!

It is not essential to spend a great deal of money on a dog bed,

but do choose one that can be easily washed. Also bear in mind that puppies chew for amusement and when they are cutting their adult teeth, so soft fabrics—and toys—may be chewed up.

Bowls

The Shih Tzu needs bowls that are not too deep. He's a relatively short-nosed breed, and dislikes having to lower his head into a bowl that then comes too close to his eyes. Get shallow food and water bowls that are not going to tip over easily. Non-spill bowls are now available from all leading pet stores. Stainless steel and heavy ceramic bowls are easy to clean and wear well. Bear in mind that with a Shih Tzu, the larger the diameter of the top of the water bowl, the wetter his face and mustache are likely to be.

Collar, leash, and ID

Your puppy's collar and leash must be secure when he goes out and about. I am always amazed at how many owners I see walking

their canine companions with collars that are far too loose. One tug backward and the collar can easily slip over the puppy's head, which could have disastrous consequences.

You must make sure that the collar is comfortable at all times, neither too tight nor too loose. Start with a good, lightweight nylon collar that can be adjusted, and a nylon leash. You should be able to place one finger between the collar and the puppy's neck. When your Shih Tzu is fully grown, you can invest in a more expensive leather collar and leash.

Your Shih Tzu must have some form of identity when he goes out in public places. Ideally, he should have an engraved tag attached to his collar with your contact details, and he should also have a permanent form of ID, such as a microchip.

Grooming equipment

Daily grooming for a Shih Tzu is essential, whether he's a pet or a show puppy. For a pet puppy, the basic grooming kit should include:

• Cotton balls to wipe around the eyes and face

• A good quality pin brush (no round tips on the pins)

• A comb with a combination of close-set and wide-set teeth

• A small, soft slicker brush (you would never use this brush on a puppy or dog that is likely to be shown)

• Guillotine or scissors type nail clippers

• Shampoo/conditioner—only use those made specifically for dogs, as others are likely to dry the coat and can cause irritation

Toys

What fun! Shih Tzu of all ages just love toys, and it is such a charming sight to watch them playing. Soft toys (fabric or soft plastic) are most certainly a favorite, and some enjoy the ones that squeak or even play tunes. However, I suspect that most of the toys have been designed to amuse the owners as well as the puppies. You will also find that your Shih Tzu is quite happy to play with inexpensive, homemade items such as the cardboard center of a toilet paper roll, or old wool socks rolled safely into a ball.

Shih Tzu usually don't enjoy extremely hard toys, and they are likely to damage the teeth.

Settling in

At long last, the time has come to bring home your Shih Tzu puppy! Try to arrange to get your puppy in the morning, so he has the rest of the day to settle into his new home. Leaving home can be a traumatic time for a puppy, so you want to make this transition as calm and stress-free as you can.

Arriving home

When you first arrive home, allow plenty of time to introduce your puppy to his new surroundings. You have already been shopping, so everything you need for your new family member is already on hand. Now you can give him your undivided attention.

The household rules that you have previously decided on will immediately come into play, as probably the first thing your puppy will need is to relieve himself. If you have decided there is a certain area in your yard to be used for this function, this should be the puppy's first place to visit.

Allow the puppy to explore his new home at his own pace, giving words of reassurance and encouragement where necessary. Even during the short trip home from the breeder, the bond between you and your new arrival has already started to form. He will look to you for guidance and confidence.

Meeting the human family

Try to avoid too much excitement when introducing the puppy to family members. By far the best and easiest way to introduce a puppy to children is to ask the children to sit quietly on the floor. A lively puppy can so easily wriggle or jump out of your arms, so to avoid any misfortunes, sitting on the floor at the puppy's level is a sensible idea.

It is important to note that when picking up your Shih Tzu (adults only!), you must hold him securely, supporting the front legs and chest with one hand and his hind legs and rear end with the other hand. Most important with this breed, always place the hind legs on the ground first when putting your dog back down, followed gently by his front legs. This prevents your Shih Tzu from jumping forward and landing painfully on his chin. A Shih Tzu, whether a puppy or an adult, can easily break his jaw by falling and landing on his chin.

Meeting the animal family

More introductions may be necessary if you have other pets in the household. A puppy generally can be somewhat pushy, so supervising the first few meetings with another pet is advisable.

If you are introducing your puppy to an established canine resident, this is best done outside the home, on neutral territory. Do not allow the puppy to take over the established dog's bed or toys, and make sure the puppy is not the only canine receiving attention, cuddling, and praise.

Supervise feeding times, making sure that each animal is eating the correct food. If necessary, separate them with a closed door, or feed the puppy inside his crate. It is also strongly recommended not to leave a new puppy alone with an older animal until you are absolutely sure all is well. No matter how good a temperament the older animal may have, a young puppy can be somewhat irritating.

A cat and a dog living in the same household can also become good friends, and may even end up sleeping together in the same bed. However, there is always the exception. When introducing a puppy or adult dog to a cat, do this indoors. The gives the cat the opportunity to retreat—by jumping onto something higher—without actually running away. This will help you to monitor what is taking place and put a stop to the dog chasing the cat.

A cat may hiss at first or even swipe; this is a normal defense mechanism. This natural, quick reaction by a cat can cause considerable damage to a puppy's face or eyes, so make sure initial interactions are supervised.

The first night

Your puppy is going to find the first night away from his litter-mates very different—it will be very quiet, and he may feel lonely. He has already experienced major changes to his daily routine, and after all this excitement he is now expected to sleep all night in a strange house, in a different bed, on his own—quite a big task for one so little!

Encourage your puppy to toilet for the last time before retiring to bed; this is going to be part of his new routine as he slowly matures to an adult. The puppy will need to feel warm and safe, and may appreciate some soft toys in his bed to cuddle up to as substitutes for his littermates.

Some people leave a nightlight on for the puppy for the first week; he may like to get accustomed to his new home before being left entirely in the dark. Others have tried a radio as company or a ticking clock. Like people, puppies are all individuals, and what works for one does not necessarily work for another. I am afraid it is a matter of trial and error.

If your puppy is sleeping in the kitchen, after making sure that his bed is comfortable, put down some newspaper a short distance from his bed, which the puppy can use for toileting during the night. Dogs do not normally soil their beds—this only happens when they have been shut in for too long in a con-fined space.

Be very positive when you leave your puppy on his own; do not linger or keep returning. This will make the situation more difficult. Try very hard not to return at every whim-per or your pup will not learn to settle.

Keep to a routine when putting your puppy to bed, so that he knows what is happening and what is expected of him—which in the long run makes him feel secure.

Housetraining

Like a human baby, a young puppy does not have a lot of control over his bladder and bowels. It can take a Shih Tzu puppy six to eight months before he is reliably housetrained. It is not advisable to let the puppy have the run of the house until you have housetraining under control.

A puppy will want to relieve himself:
- First thing in the morning
- After mealtimes

- After playing
- On waking up after a nap
- Last thing at night

A puppy will need to relieve himself at least every two hours; if you give him the opportunity at hourly intervals, this will minimize the risk of accidents.

Sometimes it is difficult to recognize when a Shih Tzu puppy squats, as

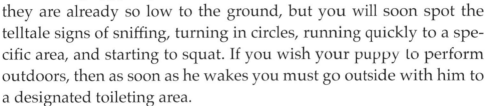

they are already so low to the ground, but you will soon spot the telltale signs of sniffing, turning in circles, running quickly to a specific area, and starting to squat. If you wish your puppy to perform outdoors, then as soon as he wakes you must go outside with him to a designated toileting area.

Most owners start off with paper training, which entails placing newspaper or puppy pads close to the door you will use for toileting trips outside. As soon as the puppy shows signs of wanting to relieve himself, put the puppy on the newspaper and stay with him, praising him lavishly when he obliges. The area covered by newspaper will need to be larger to start off with and can be reduced at a later stage, until such time as it is no longer required. Do not make the mistake of putting paper all over the house, as this is inviting the puppy to perform anywhere.

You may like to train your puppy to perform to a specific word, such as "quickly," which can be very useful in training him to relieve himself on command.

If your puppy is using a toileting area in your fenced yard, whenever possible, keep the back door open so that the puppy can go outside to perform. If this is not possible, watch your puppy and as soon as he goes to the newspaper, open the back door and take him out. Stay with the puppy, praising him as he performs.

If you wish your puppy to perform outside, no matter the weather, you must be patient. Do not put the puppy outside expecting him to perform alone. You must go out with him and stay to encourage him. After a short amount of time, and with your encouragement, you will find that as soon as you put the puppy down outside, he will dash off to his usual place and be happy to oblige.

Some owners use paper training throughout a Shih Tzu's life, as it can make life easier when it is pouring with rain or even snowing. To be able to put paper down—perhaps on the garage floor—and ask your dog to perform on command can be most helpful. While you are housetraining your puppy, pick up any rugs or mats, as these always seem like an invitation (too much like paper) to a youngster.

When accidents happen

If you are vigilant, accidents will be kept to a minimum. But should your puppy make a mistake, do not reprimand him, particularly if you discover the accident later. Your puppy will not understand why you are angry with him.

If you catch him in the act, pick him up immediately and put him straight on the paper or take him outside, praising him as he performs.

If your puppy has had an accident in the house, you must clean the area thoroughly with a product specifically made to clean up pet messes. Otherwise the odor is likely to entice the puppy to keep returnin to the same spot.

Choosing a diet

If you get your puppy from a responsible breeder, they will provide you with a diet sheet giving you the feeding instructions you need for your puppy from the time you bring him home until he is a fully grown adult. The diet sheet will also advise you of the puppy's feeding times and give you a guide to the quantity of food fed per meal.

The right food plays such an important part throughout a dog's life, but especially for a growing puppy. It is essential that your puppy receives a properly balanced diet if he is going to grow into a happy, healthy adult—and remain that way throughout his life.

Today, complete foods have been specially formulated to contain all the natural vitamins and minerals your dog requires. There is no need to add extras of any kind to these foods—in fact, you may unbalance them if you add too many extras.

Puppy feeding

Typically, a young puppy will be eating four meals a day. A puppy is very clever and will let you know when he no longer needs one of his meals by leaving it untouched. If you have any questions about feeding, or in fact anything at all to do with the puppy's welfare, do not hesitate to contact the breeder, who should be happy to help.

It is very important that the puppy remains on the diet that has been recommended by his breeder and that his digestive system is accustomed to. If there's an immediate change of diet, it is likely to cause digestive upset, possibly resulting in diarrhea. If you do decide to change the puppy's diet for any reason, always do it very gradually.

Do not give different types of food on the same day because you will not be able to tell which food agrees with your puppy and which does not. You will know from the puppy's reaction—and more particularly by the condition of the feces that he passes—whether his digestive system has coped with a new diet or not.

Do not allow your puppy to become a picky eater by giving him extra treats with his meal to tempt his appetite. The clever Shih Tzu will soon get wise to this, and will refuse to eat his food until you have added something he considers particularly appetizing.

Bones and chews

I don't believe you should give a Shih Tzu raw or cooked bones. I have worked with a veterinarian for over 30 years and have seen the sad consequences—bone splinters stuck in throats, and along the digestive tract. Also avoid rawhide bones or chews, as these become soft and may lodge in the dog's throat.

There are plenty of types of artificial bones and chews on the market that safe for your dog, such as Nylabones and those that assist in cleaning canine teeth.

If you do feel the need to give your dog something to chew on, then a good, hard dog biscuit, which is going to break up into smaller pieces and therefore be easily consumed, is a far better option.

If you intend to show your Shih Tzu, you will not be able to give him any hard item that he can chew for fear of causing damage to his face furnishings. The mustache and face furnishings of a Shih Tzu take a very long time to grow, and a considerable amount of time and effort by the owner to keep clean and ready for showing—but all can be lost in a matter of minutes!

Mealtimes

To begin with, your puppy will need four meals a day, which will all be laid down in the diet sheet given to you by the breeder. To give you a rough idea, the meals are usually given about 8 a.m., noon, 4 p.m. and 8 p.m. But of course, you may have to adjust this slightly to suit your own household.

It will not take too long before the puppy requires only three meals—usually around 16 weeks—and eventually by six to eight months only two meals a day will be necessary. Breakfast and dinner have always been appreciated by my canine companions.

Naturally, you will need to adjust the size of the meals as the puppy grows. Feeding instructions can be provided by the breeder or by the manufacturers of the dog food.

Try to keep mealtimes to a routine; feed at more or less the same times daily, in the same place, and avoid distractions while the puppy is eating. If you have more than one dog, be sure to separate them at mealtimes, feeding the same dog in the same place each time.

Do not feed your puppy or adult dog immediately before or after vigorous playing or exercise, as this can cause gas to build up in the stomach, producing extreme pain and discomfort, bloating of the stomach and even necessitating surgery.

Ideal weight

To keep your Shih Tzu in good health, it is necessary to monitor his weight. By nature, the Shih Tzu is not a greedy dog, but too many treats can alter this situation. The Shih Tzu, although robust, should not be allowed to become overweight, as carrying excess weight can cause numerous health problems, affecting the joints, the heart, and other vital organs. Puppy and adult alike should be neither too thin nor too fat. You should not be able to feel a Shih Tzu's ribs easily, but there should be a very slight indication of a waist behind the last rib.

Take care not to confuse your dog's weight with the amount of coat he has. Your Shih Tzu should be muscled, and you should not be able to feel soft, excessive fat.

Pay extra attention to the male or female Shih Tzu who has been neutered, as they need fewer calories due to the hormone changes that take place. Once they have gained weight, it is very difficult to lose.

Conversely, a Shih Tzu who is too thin is likely to be an unhealthy dog. It is a sad sight to see a dog's ribs or pin bones protruding. If you notice a drop in your dog's weight, it could be an indication of health problems. Make sure that you are feeding the correct amount of food for the active or less active dog, and that the dog has a regular worming regime in place.

The easiest way to keep on eye on your dog's weight is to weigh him regularly. Stand on the scale yourself, and record your weight. Then pick up your Shih Tzu and get on the scale again. Subtract your weight alone from the weight of you holding the dog, and you've got the dog's weight. If you're unable to do this at home, ask your veterinarian if you can stop by and put your dog on their scale. Most clinics will not charge you for this.

Chapter 6

Caring for Your Shih Tzu

The Shih Tzu is quite a robust dog, and does not make excessive demands on her owners. But her coat is a major consideration, especially if you want to keep your dog in full coat. You will need to groom to your dog every day, even if you keep her in a pet clip, as the Shih Tzu's coat grows quite quickly.

Ask the breeder to give you a demonstration of how to groom your new puppy, if possible. Or perhaps you attended a few dog shows when first studying the breed, and you picked up some grooming tips. You will learn a tremendous amount by watching someone else groom a Shih Tzu.

Once properly trained, the Shih Tzu loves being groomed and bathed because, if done correctly, she will consider it a form of affection and pampering. The secret of grooming is to start the day you bring home your puppy. This way, the puppy will learn to accept being groomed, and the coat will not get out of control.

Accustom your puppy to being groomed from an early age.

Most adult Shih Tzu love the special attention they get when they are being groomed.

If your Shih Tzu lies on her side, you will be able to get to all the awkward places.

After the coat is brushed, you will need to go over it with a wide-toothed comb.

Coat care

You can teach your Shih Tzu to lie on her side on a table so you can groom through the layers of her coat. Make sure you have a hold of her at all times while she is on the table.

At the beginning, you will find this table training a little difficult, but you will be amazed how fast she will learn. Even when she is an adult, never take the chance of having her on the table unless she is properly attended.

If at any time during the grooming your Shih Tzu becomes agitated, just stop for a moment, speak to her calmly but firmly, and begin again. Never per her down on the floor un- til you are both calm!

It is important when brushing the coat to do this properly, through all the layers, and not just brush the top coat. Be careful not to be too heavy-handed either— scratching the skin with the pins of the brush or pulling at the coat and, hence, the skin. Tease out any small mats or tan- gles between your fingers, then brush through again. You never want the groom- ing experience to hurt your dog.

To make sure that you have done the job prop- erly, it is always best to check through the coat with the wide-toothed comb.

Allow your puppy to slowly get used to and accept the brush around her head, taking great care not to touch her eyes, then go over the entire head with the wide-toothed comb. Now change to a narrow-toothed comb and comb her whiskers away from her eyes.

The topknot

Because the hair of a Shih Tzu grows particularly fast across the nose and around the eyes, it is essential to keep this hair out of the eyes to avoid any irritation or damage. In an eight-week-old puppy it is still possible to comb the hair away from the eyes, hence the importance of teaching your youngster how to be handled and groomed at that age.

By five months of age the Shih Tzu is usually ready for her first topknot, which is when the hair on the top of the head has reached sufficient length that it can be put in a special band to keep the hair out of the dog's eyes.

When putting up the topknot, the hair should be taken from the outer corner of each eye into a reverse V shape at the top of the head. Use a fabric-wrapped band that will not pull or break the hair, and won't pull it up too tight.

Coat change

If you have managed to keep a full coat on your puppy until she is about eight months old, then you are doing a really good job. However, from about 8 to 12 months the Shih Tzu starts to change her coat from a puppy coat to an adult coat. This is when owners always have the most trouble in grooming, as the baby undercoat mats so easily at this time.

Some puppies lose their puppy coats all over at the same time, whereas others seem to lose the coat in individual areas and at different speeds. No matter how much attention you give to coat care at this time, that puppy coat will change—and this is when the majority of pet owners give in and resort to having the entire coat clipped.

Clipping and trimming

Many new Shih Tzu pet owners start off with the intention of keeping their new dog in full coat, but as the weeks go by and the coat grows, it becomes apparent that, for a pet household, this is just not going to be possible.

There are other owners who never dreamed of trying to cope with a dog with so much coat, and they have already made up their minds—even before bringing home their Shih Tzu—that they would have her clipped.

Brushing out a Shih Tzu

When looking for a professional dog groomer, seek recommendations. Look for someone who is accustomed to small dogs and, even better, has actual experience with Shih Tzu. Anyone can pay to take a dog clipping and trimming course, but this does not mean that they are good at what they do. Going to the grooming salon can be very frightening for some dogs, so make sure the groomer you choose is kind and caring.

Once your dog has been clipped down, she will need to visit the groomer every two or three months.

Keeping a pet Shih Tzu in a short trimmed or scissored coat, about 2 to 3 inches (5 to 7.6 cm) long, as opposed to being clipped down, can be quite difficult. At this length the coat seems to mat easily, especially on the legs and under the armpits.

One of the most popular clipped styles is similar to a puppy look, where the coat on the body and legs is cut down quite short and the head hair is either clipped or trimmed, creating a very rounded look. The ears are trimmed to blend in with the shortened beard, and the hair remains on the tail either natural, or has been trimmed down slightly to balance the look of the dog.

Always remember that the hair close to the eyes, in particular, will grow back quite quickly. As the cut hair grows, it tends to be rather harsh and spiky and can easily irritate the eyes. Therefore, more often than not, it requires further trimming between full clips.

Bathing the pet Shih Tzu

The Shih Tzu can be bathed as often as you think necessary. It is much better to bathe your dog very regularly and not just leave it until the dog goes to the grooming salon. A clean puppy or adult is far easier to groom than a dirty dog and will be much more pleasant to have around your house.

You can start bathing from six to eight weeks of age. The first few baths may be a little awkward, but once you have mastered the technique, all will be well. Ask the pup's breeder to give you a demonstration, if possible. And be sure to use a shampoo made for the breed—shampoos for humans can dry a dog's skin.

The show dog

Correct show presentation is quite an art. A show dog needs to be bathed at least once a week and to be kept spotlessly clean and in excellent condition at all times. The head and face furnishings require daily attention.

One of the best ways to learn about this skill is to ask your dog's breeder or an experienced Shih Tzu exhibitor to demonstrate the entire procedure from beginning to end. By watching an expert, you will be able to see the right grooming equipment to use for a show dog, how the dog is bathed, conditioned, and finally blown dry.

The bathing and blow drying can take from one hour to three hours for an adult Shih Tzu in full coat. Afterward, the dog must be kept in this condition, in preparation for the show the following day.

The major part of preparing a Shih Tzu for the show ring is carried out at home. On arriving at the show, the entire coat will need to be brushed through, making sure that all has remained in order. The maintenance bands from the head furnishings can now carefully be removed, groomed and prepared for the show topknot, which is customary in the breed.

Regular checks

Your Shih Tzu will require a daily check-up, especially around the eyes, because with all their hair, it is necessary to comb the mustache away from the eyes. You can control the puppy's head by firmly holding the hair under her chin. This will also enable you to wipe any matter away from the eyes, and clean them with warm water on a cotton ball.

Eye ulcers in Shih Tzu can be so easily caused by sharp objects, a hair or hair clippings irritating the eye, resulting in severe pain and even loss of sight. It is far safer to keep the hair over the top of the nose longer and comb it away from the eyes, than to cut it short and risk the short hair protruding and damaging the eyes.

A general daily groom and check-up will take about 20 minutes, whereas leaving the coat to turn into a matted mess will not only be difficult and time consuming to put right, but also very unpleasant for all concerned. It is always best to make sure, every day, that both ends of a Shih Tzu are clean. You will find it less difficult to hose down and shampoo the rear end of a Shih Tzu and then dry it, than to try and clean it up in a half-hearted fashion. Wet wipes, a towel and talcum powder can help, until you are able to do the job properly.

Ears and nails

Not many Shih Tzu pet owners feel confident enough to cut their dogs nails or remove the hair from the inside of the dog's ears—and that is completely fine. Neither of these tasks should be attempted unless you really know what you are doing, as it is possible to do more harm than good. Seek advice from your puppy's breeder, an experienced Shih Tzu owner, or you can book an appointment with a groomer, who will do the job for you.

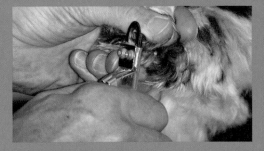

You may need help with cutting nails.

Hair growing between the pads should to be trimmed.

You may need to pluck hairs from inside the ears.

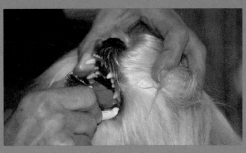

Teeth need to be cleaned regularly.

Teeth

The teeth of a Shih Tzu are quite small and not very strong; therefore, playing with toys that pull or tug is not recommended, regardless of the dog's age. A puppy is very slow to cut her teeth and can go through very uncomfortable times, with sore gums, and may breathe through her mouth instead of her nose.

Keep a check on your puppy's teeth now and throughout her life. You can train your puppy from about 10 months to have her teeth cleaned with dog toothpaste (do not use the human variety), or if

you find this too difficult there are various oral health gels and powders specially made for dogs. Your veterinarian will give you some advice about how to keep your dog's teeth healthy.

Exercising your Shih Tzu

To avoid any risk of contracting infectious diseases, you should not allow your puppy to mix with or hang out in areas used by other dogs, unless you know they are all owned and fully vaccinated pets. Ask your veterinarian when her vaccinations have conveyed full immunity. Meanwhile, you can start to train your puppy to a collar and leash in your own yard or an outside area you know is safe for her.

As an adult, this is a breed that is happy to take as much or as little exercise that you wish to give. But to begin with, as a tiny puppy, it is not sensible to walk her very far as, at this early stage, you can overstress and damage joints and ligaments. A good way of considering a puppy's exercise is to think of a human toddler and how far they are capable or happy to walk before having to be picked up.

The glory of the size of a Shih Tzu puppy is that you can walk her a little and then carry her, which enables you to get her out and about, starting to meet the world and socialize. I would stress here that you should only pick up and carry your Shih Tzu until her vaccinations are complete, or in emergencies, or else this could become a very bad habit.

The older Shih Tzu

Like elderly people, the older your Shih Tzu becomes, the more understanding, care, and attention she is likely to need and deserve. She will start to look elderly at around 10 to 12 years. Her joints may become stiff and painful with arthritis, probably her hearing will not be as good as it was, and there could be deterioration in her sight. She will be sleeping more and be less inclined to exercise; it may be necessary to change her diet to suit her changing digestive system.

Do not think that just because she is elderly, nothing can be done to help her. In fact, just the opposite applies; at this time in her life, you should have her health checked more frequently. Early detection and prompt medical assistance can add years to an elderly dog's life.

Do, however, allow her to be a senior dog, and do not expect her to do all the things she used to do. She is beginning to wind down now, so insisting that she goes for a long walk is likely to do more harm than good. Adjust her lifestyle to suit her slower pace, and try to keep to her familiar routine. A little sensible exercise is good for her, as it helps to keep her from stiffening up, stimulates her mind, increases her appetite (which is probably not as good as it was), and keeps her bowels moving, too!

Letting go

All owners dread that heartwrenching day when you must say a final farewell to your beloved Shih Tzu. If we must lose our pets, it would be slightly easier to bear if they could just quietly slip away in their sleep. Sometimes this does happen, but more often, we, as loving, responsible owners, have to make the decision to let them go. The questions nearly every owner asks are, "Is this the right time?" and, "Are we doing the right thing?"

After spending so many wonderful years with your dog, probably from a puppy through to old age, you will know her best. You will remember how she was as a youngster and what her capabilities and quality of life are in her final years.

Elderly dogs can become very distressed if they cannot stand or walk. Perhaps they are no longer clean in the house, or worse, they are in pain and life is just too much of a struggle. When this time comes and their quality of life has diminished, it will be time to let go.

Your veterinarian will help to guide you through this sad process, either at the clinic or in your own home. The vet will also be able to assist you with any specific requests and give you details regarding

cremation or a pet cemetery for your beloved companion.

All the good times and memories that you shared with your beloved Shih Tzu will stay with you forever. Taking on a new puppy or a rescued dog may help to lighten your heart. A new addition to the household will seek your attention, keep you occupied, get you out and about—and put a smile on your face. Or you might not feel ready for another dog. Do what's best for you. Whatever you decide, your life has been enriched with precious memories.

Chapter 7

Training Your Shih Tzu

Your Shih Tzu is a highly intelligent little being who is capable of learning as much as you are prepared to teach him. That said, the Shih Tzu is strong-minded and although not actually disobedient, his preference is to do what is required of him, but in his own way and at his own pace.

When you are training, it will help if you stick to the following guidelines.

• Keep training sessions short and positive. A puppy, in particular, has a short attention span and his work will deteriorate if you continue for too long.

• Make sure you reward your Shih Tzu frequently, either with treats, or maybe have a game with a favorite toy.

• Do not train after your Shih Tzu has eaten or when he has just exercised. He will be either too full or too tired to concentrate.

• Choose a training area that is free from distractions, so your Shih Tzu will focus on you.

• Try not to confuse your dog by using long sentences when only a single word is required. Remember, your Shih Tzu—clever though he is—does not speak English, so keep it simple!

• Tone of voice is more important than what you say. If you say, "Sophie, come" in a deep, gruff manner, this tone is unlikely to encourage poor Sophie. If, on the other hand, you call, "Sophie, come"' in a higher pitched, light-hearted tone, it is far more inviting. The tone of your voice is very important to your canine companion.

• If other members of your family want to get involved in training, make sure everyone uses exactly the same cues for the same actions.

• If your Shih Tzu is struggling with an exercise, go back a stage so you can reward him.

• Always end training sessions on a positive note. Training should be fun for you and your Shih Tzu.

First lessons

There are a number of basic exercises that it will be useful to teach your Shih Tzu. With a bit of patience—and bribery—it will not take him long to master them.

Wearing a collar

Collar training can begin at home, even before the puppy has finished his vaccinations. Put the collar on for about half an hour at a time so that the puppy can become accustomed

to wearing this strange object around his neck.

At first he will probably dislike the collar; he may sit still and refuse to move, or scratch at the collar and even walk backwards in an effort to try to remove it. The best way to deal with all these reactions is to distract his attention with toys or by playing with him, and all will soon be forgotten.

Allow the puppy to run around and play while wearing his collar, and slowly increase the amount of time that he is wearing it. Never leave him unsupervised with a collar on, because it can snag on something and strangle him.

It is not advisable for a Shih Tzu puppy or adult to wear a collar full time at home, unless his coat is clipped short, as it is liable to become entangled in the coat, causing problems and irritation.

Leash training

Some Shih Tzu puppies take to leash training right away, with no problems whatsoever, and off they go without a care in the world. But you may have a puppy who simply hates the leash, and when he experiences the slightest tension, he cries, lies down and refuses to budge, rolls on his back, or catapults forward in a mad burst of energy. Even this can be fixed!

The best way of introducing a Shih Tzu puppy to a leash is in his own home. Attach the leash to the puppy's collar and allow him to move around the yard with the leash trailing behind, making sure it does not get tangled up.

Dog training tips

While the leash is attached to the puppy's collar, distract him by fussing, talking, and playing with him in a very light-hearted, upbeat manner. After a few lessons, when the puppy has become accustomed to the leash, you will be able to hold the end of it.

Make sure that at first, you go where the puppy wants to go to avoid any tension on the puppy's neck. Be sure to praise your puppy for any directional moves, no matter how small they may be.

The next step is for you to go to the end of the leash and encourage your puppy to move toward you. If the puppy still refuses to move, you may need to get down to the puppy's level to begin with. But as soon as the puppy reaches you, do not forget the praise!

Unless you are planning to get involved in competitive obedience, where dogs are trained to walk on the left, it will not matter on which side of you the dog walks, but it will help if you introduce a verbal cue, such as "heel" or "walk."

Come when called

Calling your dog to come to you on cue is the most important lesson, and every dog should learn it. You will be relieved to know that

the Shih Tzu as an adult, although not the most obligingly obedient little dog, will come to you when called, although probably when he is ready.

You can start training your puppy to come as soon as he arrives in your home. He will be very responsive to you, and will want to be with you all the time. Sit on the floor, clap your hands a couple of times to attract his attention, call the puppy's name followed by "come," and presto, here he comes! Now give him plenty of praise, and maybe a treat, so that the puppy knows every time he returns to you, he is praised.

Never scold a puppy or an adult for coming to you—no matter how long he takes—or he will associate being scolded with returning to you, which will not be a great incentive.

Training can progress by adding distance and distractions. Go out into the yard and try calling your puppy. Make sure you have a really tasty treat in hand, so he learns that it is always rewarding to come when he is called.

If he is slow to respond, make yourself more exciting by using a high-pitched voice, jumping up and down, or maybe running off in the opposite direction. It does not matter how silly you look or sound, you must be irresistible to your puppy. The best form of training is when your dog thinks it is all one big game.

If a trainee is really not paying attention, you can teach this lesson with the assistance of a long light leash, which will give the puppy a gentle reminder to return to you.

Do not allow your Shih Tzu free-running exercise away from home until you are confident that he has mastered the recall.

Stationary exercises

These exercises are easy to teach, and you and your Shih Tzu will be inspired by your success!

Sit

You may have noticed that your Shih Tzu naturally sits in certain situations, such as when presented with food or a toy. If you capitalize on this, it is an excellent way to begin training.

At every opportunity, give your Shih Tzu the verbal cue "sit" when he is about to sit anyway. Make sure you only use the word "sit"—not "sit down"—as this is combining two different exercises.

To advance your training, you can use a treat, held just above your puppy's head. As he looks up at the treat, he will transfer his weight back on his hindquarters and go into the sit position. Practice this a few times, and then introduce the verbal cue.

Soon your puppy will react to the verbal cue and will not need to be lured into position. However, it is a good idea to reward your Shih Tzu now and then when he sits, to keep him on his toes!

Down

The "down" is a natural progression from "sit." Ask your puppy to "sit," making sure he knows you have a treat in your hand. Hold it in front of his nose and lower it toward the ground.

The puppy will follow the treat, often going down on his front legs to begin, followed by his hindquarters as he tries to get the treat. Keep the treat in your hand until your puppy is in the "down" position, and then reward him.

Keep practicing, and when your puppy understands what is required, introduce the verbal cue, "down." Gradually extend the time he stays down before rewarding him.

Stand

Show dogs need to learn to stand still on cue. In fact, exhibitors often choose this in preference to a "sit," as a show dog is always expected to stand in the show ring.

Training begins from as early as six weeks old, when a puppy is "stacked," which means actually putting him in the standing position required in the show ring. To begin with your puppy will try to wriggle out of position, but use a treat to help him maintain his position for just a few seconds before rewarding him.

Keep practicing, and when your puppy understands the exercise, introduce the verbal cue, "stand."

Control exercises

The Shih Tzu is full of fun and has boundless energy when he is in a playful mood. This means he can find it difficult to inhibit his behavior, but it is important to establish control, for his own safety and because everyone loves to meet a well-mannered dog, but an unruly dog is seldom welcome anywhere.

Stay

"Stay" is an extension of "sit" or "down." First put your puppy in the position you require; most dogs are more likely to remain in position in the "down," as this is most comfortable for them.

Now give a clear hand signal, with the palm of your hand toward the puppy, and take two steps to the side. Or you can face your puppy and take two steps back. Wait just a second or two, return to your pup, and praise and reward him before he has a chance to get up. Keep practicing, and then introduce the verbal cue, "stay."

Do not bend down or make direct eye contact with your puppy while teaching "stay," as this will be seen as an invitation to join you. Gradually extend the distance and the time you can leave your puppy, making sure you give lots of praise, and a treat, when the exercise is finished.

Wait

This is a word to use when you want to postpone or delay an action. Basically it means, "Stop whatever you are doing and wait until I give you the next instruction." The sound of the word "wait" should be strong and positive, to attract the attention of your puppy, placing him on standby until you deliver his next instruction.

The "wait" cue can be very useful, especially in situations where you need to keep your dog safe, such when you are opening the car door, putting on the leash, are waiting at the curb for the traffic light to change, or opening the gate. It can also be used when throwing toys for your puppy to retrieve or when putting his dinner down.

It's easiest to start teaching this cue with your dog sitting, but eventually you want him to respond from any position.

You need to differentiate "wait" from "stay" with a different hand signal. Step forward with your back to the puppy, then hold out your palm to your side, facing him. This may seem like a subtle difference, but the clever Shih Tzu will read your body language and, with practice, he will understand what is required. As he gets it, introduce the "wait" cue.

"Wait" is also a far more useful cue than "no," which has very little meaning for dogs. It's much easier to teach a dog to do something (stop whatever you are doing and wait for instructions), than to not do something (which of the many things I'm doing at the moment should I not do?). If your puppy is misbehaving or doing something dangerous, you can simply cue "wait," and then tell him what you want him to do instead: "come" or "sit," for example.

Leave it

These two words are very useful when training any breed of dog. It means, "drop that thing you have or are about to grab." You may need him to leave something particularly nasty that he finds in the street, leave a sock he has just picked up, or leave a piece of food that has fallen on the floor.

This cue can be taught quite easily when first playing with your puppy. As you gently take a toy from his mouth, introduce the verbal cue, "leave it," and then praise him. If he is reluctant, swap the toy for another toy or a treat.

Do not get involved in a tug-of-war with the puppy. Not only could this seriously damage a Shih Tzu's mouth and jaw, but also he will become over-excited and possessive, which could, if allowed to continue, teach your dog some undesirable behaviors.

The ideal Shih Tzu owner

The mistake made by many owners of small dogs is treating the dog like a pampered, spoiled child. This does the dog no favors, and it can lead to major problems when the dog fails to understand what his family wants of him.

The Shih Tzu is as bright as a button, and he will fall into bad habits as quickly as he will learn good ones. It is your job to start as you mean to go on, establishing a regime of firmness, fairness, kindness, and consistency. A dog who understands what his boundaries are will be far more content than one who is subject to the unpredictable behavior of an over-indulgent owner.

The Shih Tzu has the intelligence to learn all that you wish to teach him, but he also has the charm to be able to bring his owner around to his way of thinking! Between the two of you, compromises will be reached—but lovingly.

Chapter 8

Keeping Your Shih Tzu Busy

A lthough Shih Tzu love the comfort and security of their own home, a properly socialized dog also enjoys being out and about, meeting new people and other animals. The Shih Tzu is a very versatile breed and there are many activities owners can enjoy with their dogs, whether at a basic fun level or at a more serious competitive level. To develop and appreciate this intelligent little dog's full character and potential, you can get involved with all kinds of canine sports.

Canine Good Citizen

The American Kennel Club runs the Canine Good Citizen program. It promotes responsible ownership and helps you to train a well-behaved dog who will fit in with the community.

The program tests your dog on basic good manners, alone and with other people and dogs around. It's excellent for all pet owners

and is also an ideal starting point if you plan to compete with your Shih Tzu in any sport—including in the show ring.

Showing

At a dog show, dogs are judged against the breed standard. The dog who, in the judge's opinion, comes closest to embodying the standard takes home the ribbons.

The Shih Tzu is one of the most difficult breeds to exhibit in the show ring—this has nothing to do with any problem in the breed, but purely because of the coat care and presentation required. Over the years, presentation in the show ring has improved dramatically, and therefore to present the Shih Tzu correctly for showing requires not only time and patience, but also considerable skill.

To attain the standard at which these dogs are shown requires daily coat care, and is definitely not for the faint-hearted, nor anyone who is not prepared to keep to a proper grooming regime.

Competitive obedience

This is a sport where you are assessed as a dog and handler, completing a series of exercises including heeling, recalls, retrieves, stays, sendaways, and scent discrimination.

The Shih Tzu is not a natural obedience dog, but she is more than capable of learning and performing the exercises. These are relatively simple to begin with, involving heeling, a recall and stays in the lowest class. As you progress, more exercises are added, and the instructions you are allowed to give are reduced.

To achieve top honors in this discipline requires intensive training, as precision and accuracy are of paramount importance.

Agility

Agility is basically a canine obstacle course. It is fast and furious and is great for the fitness of both handler and dog. And it can be quite addictive! The obstacles include hurdles, long jump, tire jump, tunnels (rigid and collapsible), weaving poles, an A-frame, a dogwalk, and a seesaw.

Agility is judged on the time taken to get around the course, with faults given for knocking down fences, missing obstacles, and going through the course in the wrong order.

Puppies should not be allowed to do any agility exercises that involve jumping or contact equipment until at least 12 months old. But while you are waiting, you can begin to teach your dog how to weave, introduce him to tunnels, and play around the jumps and poles so that he becomes familiar with the equipment.

There are different size categories, and with lots of patience and positive training, the Shih Tzu can be an able agility competitor.

Canine freestyle

Also known as dancing with dogs, or musical freestyle, this activity is becoming increasingly popular with dogs of all sizes and breeds. Dog and handler perform a choreographed routine to music, allowing the dog to show off an array of tricks and moves to delight the crowd.

The Shih Tzu has the outgoing personality for this discipline, but there may be times when he takes the initiative and does a little Shih Tzu improvisation!

Flyball

Flyball is a relay race with four dogs on a team. Each dog runs down a 51-foot (15.5 m) course, jumping over four hurdles on the way to a spring-loaded box. The dog trips the lever on the box, a tennis ball pops up, the dog must catch it, and then run back over the four hurdles to the starting line. Then the next dog goes. The fastest team to have all four dogs run without errors, wins.

Small dogs are especially popular on flyball teams, because the hurdles are set at four inches below the shoulder height of the shortest dog—with eight inches (20 cm) as a minimum. Having a Shih Tzu on the team means all the dogs get those eight-inch hurdles.

Chapter 9

Health Care

We are fortunate that the Shih Tzu is a healthy dog and, with good routine care, a well-balanced diet, and sufficient exercise, most will experience few health problems. However, it is your responsibility to put a program of preventative health care in place—and this should start from the moment your puppy, or older dog, arrives in her new home.

Parasites

No matter how well you look after your Shih Tzu, you will have to accept that parasites—internal and external—are ever present, and you need to take preventive action.

Internal parasites live inside your dog. These are the various worms. Most will find a home in the digestive tract, but there is also a parasite that lives in the heart. If infestation is unchecked, a dog's health will be severely jeopardized, but routine preventive treatment is simple and effective.

External parasites live on your dog's body—in her skin and fur, and sometimes in her ears.

Roundworm

This is found in the small intestine. Signs of infestation will be a poor coat, a potbelly, diarrhea, and lethargy. Prospective mothers should be treated before mating, but it is almost inevitable that parasites she may have will be passed on to the puppies. For this reason, a breeder will start a worming program, which you will need to continue. Ask your vet for advice on treatment, which will need to continue throughout your dog's life.

 Vaccinating Your Dog

The American Animal Hospital Association and the American Veterinary Medical Association have issued vaccination guidelines that apply to all breeds of dogs. They divide the available vaccines into two groups: core vaccines, which every dog should get, and non-core vaccines, which are optional.

Core vaccines are canine parvovirus-2, distemper, and adenovirus-2. Puppies should get vaccinated every three to four weeks between the ages of 6 and 16 weeks, with the final dose at 14 to 16 weeks of age. If a dog older than 16 weeks is getting their first vaccine, one dose is enough. Dogs who received an initial dose at less than 16 weeks should be given a booster after one year, and then every three years or more thereafter.

Rabies is also a core vaccine. For puppies less than 16 weeks old, a single dose should be given no earlier than 12 weeks of age. Revaccination is recommended annually or every three years, depending on the vaccine used and state and local laws.

Non-core vaccines are canine parainfluenza virus, Bordetella bronchiseptica, canine influenza virus, canine measles, leptospirosis, and Lyme disease. The dog's exposure risk, lifestyle, and geographic location all come into play when deciding which non-core vaccines may be appropriate for your dog. Have a conversation with your veterinarian about the right vaccine protocol for your dog.

Tapeworm

Infection occurs when the dog ingests fleas or lice. The adult worm takes up residence in the small intestine, releasing mobile segments (which contain eggs), which can be seen in a dog's feces as small rice-like grains. The only other obvious sign of infestation is irritation of the anus. Again, routine preventive treatment is required throughout your dog's life.

Heartworm

This parasite is transmitted by mosquitoes, and is found in all parts of the USA, although its prevalence does vary. Heartworms live in the right side of the heart and larvae can grow up to 14 inches (35 cm) long. A dog with heartworm is at severe risk from heart failure, so preventive treatment, as advised by your vet, is essential. Dogs should also have regular tests to check for the presence of infection.

Lungworm

Lungworm is a parasite that lives in the heart and major blood vessels supplying the lungs. It can cause many problems, such as breathing difficulties, excessive bleeding, sickness, diarrhea, seizures, and even death. The dog becomes infected when ingesting slugs and snails, often accidentally when rummaging through undergrowth. Lungworm is not common, but it is on the increase and a responsible owner should be aware of it. Fortunately, it is easily preventable, and even affected dogs usually make a full recovery if treated early enough. Your vet will be able to advise you on the risks in your area and what form of treatment may be required.

Fleas

A dog may carry many types of fleas. The flea stays on the dog only long enough to feed and breed, but its presence will result in itching. If your dog has an allergy to fleas—usually a reaction to the flea's saliva—she will scratch herself until she is raw. Spot-ons and chewable flea preventives are easy to use and highly effective, and should be given regularly to prevent fleas. Some also prevent ticks.

If your dog has fleas, talk to your veterinarian about the best treatment. Bear in mind that your entire home, dog's whole environment, and all other pets in your home will also need to be treated.

How to Detect Fleas

You may suspect your dog has fleas, but how can you be sure? There are two methods to try.

Run a fine comb through your dog's coat, and see if you can detect the presence of fleas on the skin, or clinging to the comb. Alternatively, sit your dog on some white paper and rub his back. This will dislodge feces from the fleas, which will be visible as small brown specks. To double check, shake the specks on to some damp cotton. Flea feces consists of the dried blood taken from the host, so if the specks turn a lighter shade of red, you know your dog has fleas.

Ticks

These are blood-sucking parasites that are most frequently found in areas where sheep or deer are present.

The main danger is their ability to pass a wide variety of very serious diseases—including Lyme disease—to both dogs and humans. The preventive you give your dog for fleas generally works for ticks, but you should discuss the best product to use with your veterinarian.

Ear mites

These parasites live in the outer ear canal. The signs of infestation are a brown, waxy discharge, and your dog will often shake her head and scratch her ear.

If you suspect your dog has ear mites, a visit to the vet will be needed so that medicated ear drops can be prescribed.

Common ailments

As with all living animals, dogs can be affected by a variety of ailments, most of which can be treated effectively after consulting with your vet, who will prescribe appropriate medication and will advise you on how to care for your dog's needs.

Here are some of the more common problems that could affect your Shih Tzu, with advice on how to deal with them.

Anal glands

These are two small sacs on either side of the anus, which produce a dark brown secretion. The anal glands should empty every time a dog defecates, but if they become blocked or impacted, a dog will experience increasing discomfort. She may lick at her rear end, or scoot her bottom along the ground to relieve the irritation.

Treatment involves a trip to the vet, who will empty the glands manually. It is important to do this without delay or they could become infected.

Dental problems

The Shih Tzu can be prone to dental problems, and good dental hygiene will do much to minimize problems with gum infection and tooth decay.

If tartar accumulates to the extent that you cannot remove it by brushing, your dog will need to be anesthetized for a dental cleaning by the veterinarian.

How to Remove a Tick

If you spot a tick on your dog, do not try to pluck it off, as you risk leaving the hard mouth parts embedded in his skin. The best way to remove a tick is to use a fine pair of tweezers, or you can buy a tick remover. Grasp the tick head firmly and then pull the tick straight out from the skin. If you are using a tick remover, check the instructions, as some recommend a circular twist when pulling. When you have removed the tick, clean the area with mild soap and water.

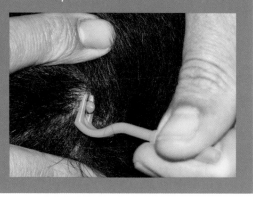

Diarrhea

There are many reasons why a dog has diarrhea, but most commonly it is the result of scavenging, a sudden change of diet, or an adverse reaction to a particular type of food.

If your dog is suffering from diarrhea, the first step is to withhold food for a day. It is important that she does not become dehydrated, so make sure that fresh drinking water is available. However, drinking too much can increase the diarrhea, which may be accompanied with vomiting, so limit how much she drinks at any one time.

After allowing the stomach to rest, feed a bland diet, such as white fish or chicken with boiled rice for a few days. In most cases, your dog's motions will return to normal and you can resume normal feeding, although this should be done gradually.

However, if this fails to work and the diarrhea persists for more than a few days, you should consult your vet. Your dog may have an infection, which needs to be treated with antibiotics, or the diarrhea may indicate some other problem that needs expert diagnosis.

Ear infections

The Shih Tzu has long feathering on her ears, so air will not circulate as easily as it would in dogs with semi-pricked or pricked ears. This means that a Shih Tzu is more prone to ear infections.

A healthy ear is clean, with no sign of redness or inflammation, and no evidence of a waxy brown discharge or a foul odor. If you see your dog scratching her ear, shaking her head, or holding one ear at an odd angle, you will need to consult your vet. The most likely causes are ear mites, an infection, or there may be a foreign body, such as a grass seed, trapped in the ear.

Depending on the cause, treatment is with medicated ear drops, possibly containing antibiotics. If a foreign body is suspected, the vet will need to carry out further investigations.

Eye problems

The Shih Tzu has shallow eye sockets and prominent eyes, which means the eyeballs are more vulnerable than in other breeds. It is not unusual for the eye to be injured by a thorn, or some other sharp object, so take care where you exercise your dog.

If your Shih Tzu's eyes look red and sore, she may be suffering from conjunctivitis. This may or may not be accompanied by a watery or a crusty discharge. Conjunctivitis can be caused by a bacterial or viral infection, it could be the result of an injury, or it may be a reaction to pollen.

You will need to consult your veterinarian for a correct diagnosis, but in the case of an infection, treatment with medicated eye drops is effective.

Conjunctivitis may also be the first sign of more serious inherited eye problems, which will be discussed later in this chapter.

Heatstroke

The Shih Tzu is a brachyce-phalic breed, like the Pekingese, Bulldog, Pug, and Lhasa Apso. All these dogs have a shorter muzzle than most dog breeds, and a flatter nose. Although this feature should not be exaggerated, it does mean these breeds may have more labored breath-ing and, as a result, they will overheat more easily.

Shih Tzu skin issues

On warm days, make sure your dog always has access to shady areas, and wait for a cooler part of the day before going for a walk. Never leave your Shih Tzu in a parked car, as the temperature can rise dramatically—even on a cloudy day. Heatstroke can happen very rapidly, and unless you are able lower your dog's temperature, it can be fatal.

The signs of heatstroke include heavy panting and difficulty breathing, bright red tongue and mucous membranes, thick saliva, and vomiting. Eventually, the dog becomes progressively unsteady and passes out.

If your dog appears to be suffering from heatstroke, this is a true emergency. Lie her flat and then cool her as quickly as possible by hosing her or covering her with wet towels. As soon as she has made some recovery, take her to the vet.

Lameness or limping

There are a wide variety of reasons why a dog might go lame, from a simple muscle strain to a fracture, ligament damage, or more complex problems with the joints, including inherited disorders. It takes an expert to make a correct diagnosis, so if you are concerned about your dog, do not delay in seeking help.

As your dog becomes elderly, she may suffer from arthritis, which you will see as general stiffness, particularly when she gets up after resting. It will help if you ensure her bed is in a warm, draft-free location, and if your Shih Tzu gets wet after exercise, be sure to dry her thoroughly.

If your elderly dog seems to be in pain, consult your vet, who will be able to help with pain relief medication and nutritional supplements.

Skin problems

If your dog is scratching or nibbling at her skin, first check for fleas. There are also other external parasites that cause itching and hair loss, but you will need a vet to help you find the culprit.

An allergic reaction is another major cause of skin problems. It can be hard to find the cause of the allergy, and you will need to follow your vet's advice, which often requires eliminating specific ingredients from the diet, as well as looking at environmental factors.

Inherited disorders

There are a number of conditions that can be passed on from one generation to the next, and there are some disorders that a particular breed will be more likely to inherit. If your dog is diagnosed with any of the diseases listed here, it is important to remember that they can affect offspring, so it is not wise to breed affected dogs. There are now recognized screening tests that enable breeders to check for carrier and affected individuals, and hence reduce the prevalence of these diseases within the breed. DNA testing is also becoming more

widely available, and as research into genetic diseases progresses, more DNA tests are being developed.

Although breeders strive to eliminate these problems from their bloodlines, it is important to research the breed thoroughly before buying a puppy.

Eye problems

The Shih Tzu is predisposed to a number of inherited eye conditions, and some are due to the structure of her skull. As mentioned earlier, brachycephalic breeds have a shortened muzzle and shallow eye sockets, which makes the eyes more prominent. In some dogs, this can result in an inability to completely close both eyelids over the eye. This can cause a condition known as exposure keratitis, which causes inflammation and ulceration of the cornea.

The Shih Tzu can also suffer from proptosis, where the eyelids clamp shut behind the eyeball, cutting off the blood supply to the retina. This is a real emergency and urgent veterinary help must be sought in order to save the eye.

Cataracts cloud the lens of your dog's eyes. They can appear in either or both eyes. Because Shih Tzu are genetically predisposed to developing cataracts, they can show up in relatively young dogs. Some cataracts are small and do not grow, some grow slowly, but others can render your dog blind in a short time. The Companion

Animal Eye Registry (CAER) recommends annual eye testing.

Entropion is an in-turning of the eyelids, which means the eyeball is often irritated by in-growing eyelashes. Surgical correction is generally successful.

A dog with distichiasis has a double row of eyelashes, and one or both may rub on the surface of the cornea. Surgical removal of the eyelashes is usually required.

Keratoconjunctivitis sicca, also known as dry eye, occurs when there is inadequate tear production. The eye becomes dry and itchy; the cornea may become ulcerated or scarred, resulting in loss of vision. Treatment is aimed at stimulating the tear glands, and administering artificial tears for the rest of the dog's life.

Progressive retinal atrophy is a degeneration of the eye nerves, which starts as night blindness and deteriorates to full blindness. There is no treatment. Dogs can be cleared by CAER before breeding.

Brachycephalic Airway Syndrome

Short-faced breeds such as Shih Tzu can have a variety of breathing problems that fall under this general heading. The most common problems seen in Shih Tzu are collapsed trachea (an abnormality in the rings of the trachea can cause it to collapse), elongated palate (the soft tissue at the back of the roof of the mouth grows too long for the head and can block the trachea), and stenotic nares (very narrow nostrils). Changes in lifestyle and medication may help in managing these breathing problems. Sometimes, surgery is recommended.

Patellar Luxation

This is an orthopedic problem, where the dog's kneecap slips out of place because of anatomical deformities in the joint. Treatment involves rest and anti-inflammatory medications. In more severe cases, surgery may be the best option. The Orthopedic Foundation for Animals (OFA) grades the degree of luxation or certifies that a dog is clear, based on X-rays.

Hypothyroidism

Dogs with this condition have an overactive thyroid gland, which can cause hair loss, lethargy, and weight gain—and eventually, if untreated, death. The problem is more common with older dogs. It can be treated with surgery and medication.

Summing up

This has been a long list of health problems, but it was not my intention to scare you. Acquiring some basic knowledge is an asset, as it will allow you to spot signs of trouble at an early stage. Early diagnosis very often leads to the most effective treatment.

Fortunately, the Shih Tzu is a generally healthy and disease-free dog, and annual check-ups will be all she needs. In most cases, you can look forward to enjoying many happy years with this affectionate and highly entertaining companion.

Find Out More

Books

Bradshaw, John, *Dog Sense: How the New Science of Dog Behavior Can Make You a Better Friend to Your Pet*. New York: Basic Books, 2014.

Eldredge, Debra M., DVM, Liisa D. Carlson, DVM, Delbert G. Carlson, DVM, and James M. Giffin, MD, *Dog Owner's Home Veterinary Handbook*, 4th Ed. New York: Howell Book House, 2007.

Eldredge, Debra, DVM, and Kate Eldredge, *Idiot's Guides: Dog Tricks*. New York: Alpha, 2015.

Stilwell, Victoria, *Train Your Dog Positively: Understand Your Dog and Solve Common Behavior Problems Including Separation Anxiety, Excessive Barking, Aggression, Housetraining, Leash Pulling, and More!* Berkeley: Ten Speed Press, 2013.

Websites

www.allshihtzu.com All Shih Tzu

www.akc.org American Kennel Club

www.americanshihtzuclub.org American Shih Tzu Club

www.petmd.com PetMD

www.usshihtzurescue.org Shih Tzu Rescue

www.ukcdogs.com United Kennel Club

agility in this case, a canine sport in which dogs navigate an obstacle course

breed standard a detailed written description of the ideal type, size, shape, colors, movement, and temperament of a dog breed

conforms aligns with, agrees with

docked cut or shortened

dysplasia a structural problem with the joints, when the bones do not fit properly together

heatstroke a medical condition in which the body overheats to a dangerous degree

muzzle (n) the nose and mouth of a dog; (v) to place a restraint on the mouth of a dog

neuter to make a male dog unable to create puppies

parasites organisms that live and feed on a host organism

pedigree the formal record of an animal's descent, usually showing it to be purebred

socialization the process of introducing a dog to as many different sights, sounds, animals, people and experiences as possible, so he will feel comfortable with them all

spay to make a female dog unable to create puppies

temperament the basic nature of an animal, especially as it affects their behavior

Index